THE BOULTON
PAUL BALLIOL

THE BOULTON PAUL BALLIOL

THE LAST MERLIN-POWERED AIRCRAFT

ALEC BREW

FONTHILL

Flt Lt Alexander Ewart 'Ben' Gunn test-flying a prototype Boulton Paul Balliol.

Fonthill Media Limited
Fonthill Media LLC
www.fonthillmedia.com
office@fonthillmedia.com

First published in the United Kingdom and the United States of America 2015

British Library Cataloguing in Publication Data:
A catalogue record for this book is available from the British Library

Typeset in 10.5pt on 13pt Sabon
Printed and bound in England

Contents

The prototype of the Percival Prentice, the RAF's new post-war basic trainer. The Pretence and Balliol were to be the RAF's new flight training team.

Acknowledgements

When I was writing the history of Boulton Paul Aircraft in 1991, the then Managing Director of the company, Paul Strothers, gave me permission to make whatever use I wished of its surviving archives, which included 20,000 negatives. It was at that time that I made prints of many of the illustrations which appear in this book. Boulton Paul's former Chief Test Pilot, 'Ben' Gunn, also gave me a great deal of information about the aircraft, with which he will always be associated. I am also grateful to Mark Ansell for passing on many other Balliol photographs which he came across over the years. I particularly want to thank Wendy Matthiason for putting up with having pieces of Balliol lying around our house for the last twenty years, which, as I write, includes the half-restored throttle quadrant of WN534 next to the washing machine!

Pre-production Balliol on air-test near the Boulton Paul factory, flown by A. E. 'Ben' Gunn.

'Leader's Benefit', Balliols in service with No. 7 FTS at RAF Cottesmore.

Introduction

Boulton Paul Aircraft was the company that built the Balliol, Britain's last aircraft to be powered by the iconic Rolls-Royce Merlin engine. This manufacturer went through four major phases in the near 100 years that it contributed to the aircraft industry. Boulton Paul was famous for superlative twin-engine medium bombers, then for building two-seat fighters, then for power-operated gun turrets and a military trainer, the Balliol, and finally for powered flying controls.

In 1915, the 120-year-old Boulton & Paul Ltd of Norwich most distinguished for its wooden constructions—though also involved in steelwork and engine building among other things—was brought into aircraft manufacture by the government. It was awarded contracts to build FE.2B/Ds and then Sopwith Camels, and in fact built more Camels than any other manufacturer.

Two years later, with Camels rolling off the production line at a rate of up to seventy per week, Boulton & Paul's directors decided to launch their own design department. To head it, they recruited John Dudley North as Chief Engineer, a young man who had made a name for himself designing aircraft at the Graham White Company at Hendon, and then opening aircraft production lines at Austin Motors. After building the unsuccessful Bobolink fighter and the experimental P.6, Boulton & Paul made a name for itself in metal construction and a number of superlative high-speed twin-engine medium bombers—the Bourges, Bolton, Bodmin, and Bugle—but no production orders were forthcoming. The RAF was an advocate of the slow, heavy night bomber, and if it were to order medium bombers at all, these would have to have a single engine, like the Hawker Horseley.

Boulton & Paul did win the contract to build the metal frame of the largest aircraft ever built in Great Britain—the R.101 airship—and tried its hand at other types, of course—the odd fighter, light aircraft, heavy bomber, and airliner. However, few orders were issued beyond the prototypes. Finally, the next Boulton & Paul medium bomber in the series, the Sidestrand, won orders of eighteen examples, to equip No. 101 Squadron; and when it came to re-equipment, the squadron placed an order for twenty-four of its successor, the Overstrand.

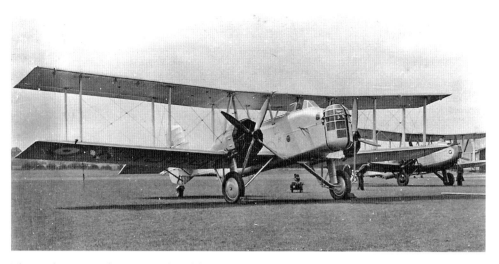

The Boulton & Paul Overstrand, and behind it its predecessor, the Sidestrand.

The Overstrand was the catalyst for a complete change in the company's trajectory. It was basically a Sidestrand with more powerful engines, and, crucially, the world's first fully enclosed power-operated gun turret for the nose gunner or bomb aimer and his single Lewis gun. In 1934, the aircraft department of Boulton & Paul was sold off to an investment company, and moved to a brand new factory in Wolverhampton in 1936, rebranded Boulton Paul Aircraft Ltd. The Overstrand was the last design built in Norwich and from then on, two-seat single-engine fighters filled the new factory, beginning with 105 Hawker Demons.

Because of the appearance of the Overstrand, North was contacted by a French company, SAMM, about its design of an electro-hydraulic four-gun turret. North immediately spotted its potential, and bought the rights to build it as the armament for a new two-seat turret fighter, and what would become the company's most famous product—the Defiant. With orders for Defiants totalling 1,062, Boulton Paul also received contracts to build the Blackburn Roc, which had won the contest to become the naval turret fighter. Blackburn Aircraft's resources were stretched during construction of the Skua and preparation for production of the Botha, so it awarded the contract to build 136 Rocs to Boulton Paul, which was already supplying its gun turret.

Boulton Paul therefore found itself upgrading from one production line of one two-seat fighter—the Demon—to two—the Defiant and Roc—side by side. But proposals to build their replacements came to naught, and the factory accommodated the production of the Fairey Barracuda instead. For a time North turned his attention to naval aircraft, but all that came of it was an order for 100 Hawker Sea Furies. The first was nearly complete when the war ended, but the order was cancelled, together with the remaining orders for the Barracuda.

Over 20,000 Boulton Paul gun turrets had been built during the war, after which their production continued. However, North had already decided that, in the post-

A Defiant being test-flown by Colin Evans near the factory.

war era, the best option for a company the size of Boulton Paul was to build military trainers. The first official requirement to attract his attention was Spec. T.23/43, which called for a new elementary trainer to replace the wartime Tiger Moths and Magisters. It was to feature a revolutionary new seating arrangement, with student and instructor side by side, and a third seat behind for another student, to observe how his compatriot got on.

The three-seat concept had been tested in 1944 with a Miles M-28, which was fitted with three sets of controls: students sat side by side, and the instructor in the back with controls which could override them. This layout did not have much to recommend it, however; in the new trainers, one of the front seats was reserved for the instructor, and there were no controls in the back, where the second student would simply observe.

Boulton Paul drew up three related designs: the P.106A, with side-by-side seating for two; the P.106B, basically the same but with the required third seat; and the P.106C, with a much narrower fuselage and tandem seating for two, the instructor being in a slightly raised seat. All three versions were offered with a choice of engines: either the 210-hp De Havilland Gipsy Queen II or the 200-hp Gipsy Queen III. The design was very simple, and included constant chord and V struts, as well as a strut-braced fixed undercarriage. The tail feathers were quite unusual, for there was no fixed fin or tail plane, and the three all-moving surfaces were interchangeable.

A model of the Boulton Paul P.106 basic trainer proposal.

The order for the RAF's new trainer went to the rather more powerful Percival Prentice. Percival Aircraft was another company, of about Boulton Paul's size, which saw its future in the production of military trainers.

Boulton Paul then turned its attention to Spec. T.7/45, an offshoot of Official Requirement No. 215, which outlined the need for a new advanced trainer to replace the wartime Harvards and Masters. It too was to have a three-seat layout, but was uncommon in that it had to be powered by one of the new turboprop engines—though, as a back-up, it also had to be capable of being fitted with the Bristol New Perseus radial engine.

There were two 1,000-hp turboprops then under development: the Armstrong-Siddeley Mamba and the Rolls-Royce Dart. Boulton Paul chose the latter for its initial submission, the P.108.

1

The P.108 Balliol

The original design of the P.108 was very different from the aircraft in its final form. Apart from the Dart engine, which was never in fact fitted, there remained the third, starboard-facing seat. It had no all-round vision, since the canopy was faired into the rear fuselage. The alternative New Perseus engine version was largely similar, and designated the P.109.

By the time that a mock-up of the P.108 had been built, the design had changed significantly: the third seat was placed in the centre, facing forward, and an all-round vision canopy was fitted with a marked step at the rear. The Rolls-Royce Dart remained the preferred engine, though neither it nor the Mamba had yet been built.

There were four submissions for the Spec. T.7/45 requirement: the P.108, the Avro Type 701, the Blackburn B.52, and the Miles M.70. Two of them received orders for four prototypes—the P.108, which was named Balliol after the Oxford college, and the Avro Type 701, which was named Athena. Boulton Paul's aircraft were allotted the serials VL892, VL917, VL935, and VL954.

Because neither of the turboprop engines had yet achieved their 100-hour type test, it was proposed that the first Balliol prototype be fitted with a Bristol Mercury engine so that flight trials could begin—the Mercury was the engine for which a minimum amount of changes were required. The P.108 was an all-metal stressed-skin aircraft with a circular fuselage section fore and aft of the roomy cockpit, itself at the structural heart of the airframe and with the inner wings bolted to it. It was designed to be a rugged aircraft with a strengthened lower fuselage, for instance, able to withstand a wheels-up landing with minimal damage. It also had interchangeable fin and tail planes, ailerons, and elevators in the manner of the P.106, to minimise spares holdings. The main oleo-pneumatic undercarriage legs were also interchangeable and of Boulton Paul design, the company having been one of their pioneers. The legs were housed in special box structures, self-contained, and profiled to form part of the wing leading edge. They were held in place by just four dowel units, making the replacement of a complete undercarriage leg a quick and simple matter. The tail wheel was fully castoring and steerable from the rudder,

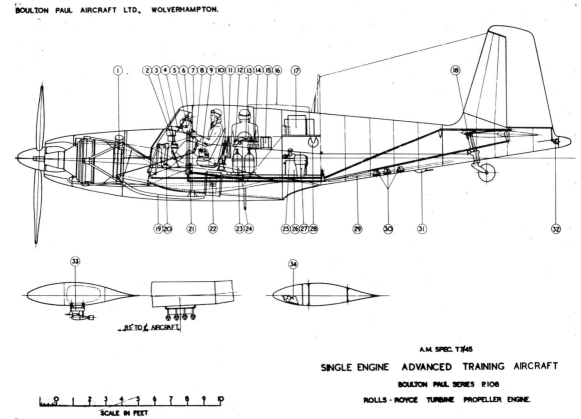

A.M. SPEC. T7/45

SINGLE ENGINE   ADVANCED   TRAINING   AIRCRAFT

BOULTON PAUL SERIES P.108

ROLLS - ROYCE   TURBINE   PROPELLER   ENGINE.

SCALE IN FEET.

The original P.108 proposal with the third seat facing starboard, Dart engine, and the faired-in canopy.

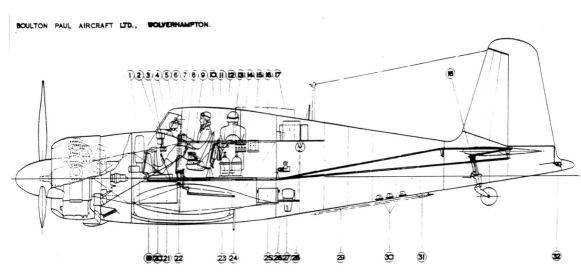

Side view of the parallel P.109 proposal.

BOULTON PAUL AIRCRAFT LTD, WOLVERHAMPTON.

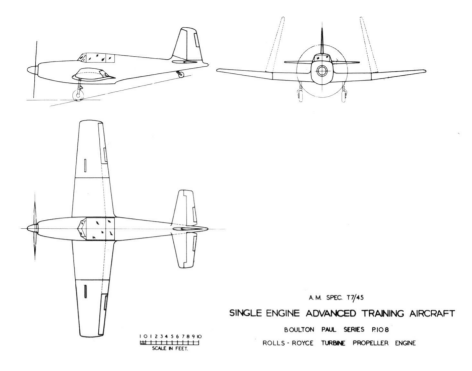

A.M. SPEC. T7/45

SINGLE ENGINE ADVANCED TRAINING AIRCRAFT

BOULTON PAUL SERIES P.108

ROLLS - ROYCE TURBINE PROPELLER ENGINE

I 0 I 2 3 4 5 6 7 8 9 10
SCALE IN FEET.

Above: Three-view drawing of the original P.108 proposal.

Right: Three-view drawing of the P.109.

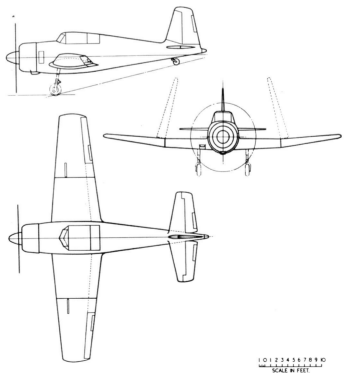

I 0 I 2 3 4 5 6 7 8 9 10
SCALE IN FEET.

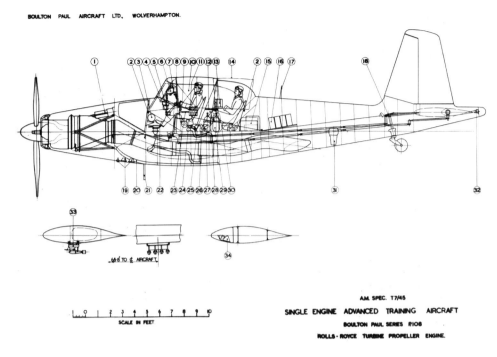

BOULTON   PAUL   AIRCRAFT   LTD.,   WOLVERHAMPTON.

SCALE IN FEET

A.M. SPEC. T7/45

SINGLE ENGINE   ADVANCED   TRAINING   AIRCRAFT

BOULTON PAUL SERIES P108

ROLLS · ROYCE   TURBINE   PROPELLER   ENGINE.

Revised layout for the Boulton Paul P.108, with third seat facing forward and an all-round vision canopy, but still the Dart engine.

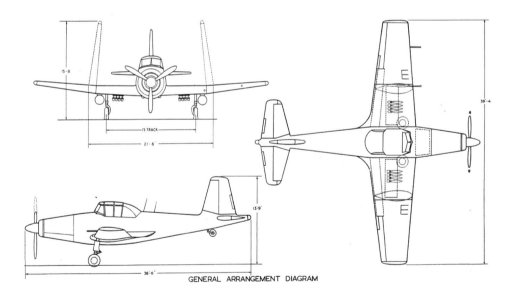

GENERAL   ARRANGEMENT   DIAGRAM

Final general arrangement drawing for the P.108 from the Boulton Paul brochure.

Above and below: The P.108 mock-up showing the stepped rear canopy and provision for drop tanks.

with a lock to fix it fore and aft, for take-off and landing. A glider towing hook was fitted to the very rear of the fuselage, which could also be used to tow targets.

There were no hydraulics on the aircraft, apart from a small motor to work the windscreen wipers; everything was operated pneumatically, with a basketball-sized spherical reservoir in the lower fuselage. It was believed that pneumatics were easier for servicing, and were in any case further aided by forty access panels, attached with quick release fasteners all over the airframe. The jet pipe ran under the cockpit floor and exhausted on the starboard side of the rear fuselage to counteract propeller torque.

In August 1946, both Boulton Paul and Avro received orders for twenty pre-production aircraft, to be powered by either of the new turboprops. Boulton Paul proposed to install ten with the Mamba and ten with the Dart, but as the Armstrong-Siddeley design was then in a more advanced stage of development, it was decided to fit the Mamba to the four prototypes.

As even the Mamba would not be ready by the time VL892's airframe was complete, Boulton Paul went ahead and initially fitted the 820-hp Bristol Mercury radial. Miles Martinet RG907 was flown in to Pendeford, and its entire power-egg, engine, cowlings, and propeller were removed and fitted to VL892.

In this form VL892 flew for the first time from Wolverhampton Airport at Pendeford on 26 May 1947, with Boulton Paul's Chief Test Pilot, Robin Lindsay Neale, at the controls. Neale had been a test pilot at the manufacturer's since before the war, and had replaced Cecil Feather as Chief Test Pilot upon the latter's retirement in 1945. The third seat was not fitted at the time of the test flight; in fact, no Balliol ever flew with the third seat, for the whole concept was quietly brushed aside.

Also under consideration was the idea of equipping the P.108 with turboprop engines. These were proving difficult to develop, and were expensive, besides. Other engines were considered, including the Rolls-Royce Merlin, the New Perseus, and its stablemate the Pegasus, and in June 1947 the Air Ministry decided that production Balliols would be fitted with war-surplus Merlins. The mark chosen was the Mk.27, a Hurricane engine, of which a large number of unused examples were in storage. They were to be overhauled and de-rated to 1,250 hp by Rolls-Royce, in order to give them longer life between overhauls. The result was the Mk.35.

Although Boulton Paul's four prototypes were still meant to be powered by the Mamba engine, the pre-production order was later amended, and the fourth model, VL954, cancelled entirely. There would from then on be four Merlin-engine prototypes, VW897 to VW900, followed by seventeen pre-production aircraft, VR590 to VR606. Thus, a total of twenty-four prototypes and pre-production aircraft were retained. The three Mamba-powered prototypes were designated the Balliol T.1, and those powered by Merlins the Balliol T.2. Orders for the Avro Athena were altered in the same manner.

With VL892 still flying with the Mercury, the first Mamba-powered Balliol was to be VL917, which became the World's first single-engine turboprop to fly, beating the rival Athena by two weeks. The first turboprop of all was the twin-engine Gloster Trent-Meteor.

The maiden flight of VL917 was again piloted by Neale from Wolverhampton Airport, and on 24 May 1948, company photographer Jack Endean filmed the aircraft taxiing out on this historic first. He began filming again 20 minutes later, as the aircraft came in to land at the eastern end of the airfield. Unfortunately, the propeller disced—turned across the airflow and acted like an airbrake—thus dragging the aircraft out of the air, and the undercarriage clipped the iron railings along the Marsh Lane boundary. The aircraft crashed onto the airfield and broke into several pieces, all the while captured on film. Neale broke his leg in the crash—the same leg that he had broken in a motor-cycle accident before the war, and which had already given him a permanent limp.

The first Avro Athena, VM125, flew on 12 June and was powered by the Mamba. No interim piston engine was fitted to it, and this might well have been why it was always just a little behind the Balliol in its development. The second, Dart-powered Athena prototype first flew on 17 July 1949, and the third, Mamba-powered Athena T.1, on 12 December 1949.

The third Balliol T.1 prototype, VL935, was moved to Armstrong-Siddeley's airfield at Bitteswell, to take advantage of its longer runways. The Armstrong-Siddeley Chief Test Pilot, Sqn Ldr Price-Owen, made the aircraft's first flight on 27 May 1948. As VL917's maiden voyage had ended in a crash, this may be considered the world's first successful flight of a single-engine turboprop, having still beaten the Athena T.1 to the air.

The first prototype had continued to be used for airframe trials, at one point fitted with anhedral wingtips, as had the new, more streamlined rear canopy which initially had a metal rear portion and was eventually all glazed. The first prototype was then fitted with the Mamba engine in 1949, while the Mercury was re-fitted to the Martinet kept in the flight shed. VL892 went to A Squadron's Aeroplane and Armament Experimental Establishment (A&AEE) at Boscombe Down for handling checks on 4 June 1952, and was then transferred to the Empire Test Pilots School on 17th June, where it was used for turboprop handling experience. Finally, it became an instructional airframe at RNAS Arbroath from April 1954 onwards, and ended its days there.

Meanwhile, the first Merlin-powered prototype, VW897, was being prepared at Pendeford, Wolverhampton. The slim, tapered nose of the T.1 was replaced by a more pugnacious one to accommodate the Merlin engine and its chin radiator. The hole for the jet pipe in the rear side of the fuselage was covered with an inspection panel, which was retained on all Balliols. The fuel tank in the upper forward fuselage was replaced by a cylindrical 25-gallon tank in the lower forward fuselage, where the jet pipe used to run. The two 50-gallon wing tanks remained, able to slide in and out of the wings when these were folded. Folding the wings was manually possible on all Balliols: it required two men to push up on the wing-tip while two others on the opposite wing hauled the wing up with a rope, and secured it with a jury strut.

Balliol T.1 VL892 outside the Boulton Paul flight sheds during the bitterly cold spring of 1947.

VL892 in the air, photographed from the company's Airspeed Oxford G-AHTW.

Robin Lindsay Neal making a low pass across Pendeford Airfield in VL892.

VL892 being flown by Robin Lindsay Neale near to the factory.

VL892 air-to-air, showing the non-enclosed main wheels.

Robin Lindsay Neale about to test-fly a Defiant during the war.

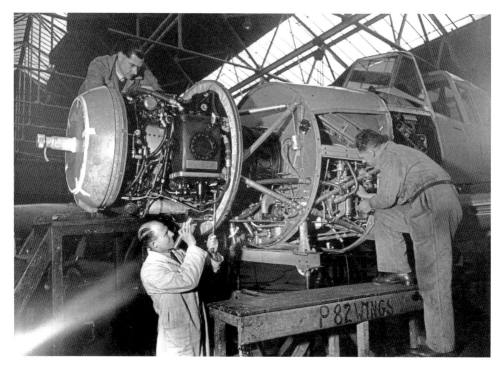

VL917 under construction with trestles which had been used for Defiant wings.

Final assembly of VL917, the second Balliol T.1 prototype.

VL917 outside the flight sheds before its first flight.

VL917 ready for its first flight in May 1948.

VL917 with one of the Wellingtons which were being converted into T.10s by Boulton Paul at the time.

Robin Lindsay Neale taxiing VL917 out for its first flight.

These pages and overleaf: Various views of the crash of VL917 after its historic first flight.

The cockpit of VL917 showing a spade grip on the starboard control column, and a handlebar grip to port, as well as extra instrumentation above the windscreen.

The first Mamba-powered Athena prototype, VM125, at the Society of British Aerospace Companies (SBAC) Show in 1948.

Avro Athena prototype VM132.

The third Balliol prototype, VL935, being assembled at Bitteswell.

VL935 in the air.

VL892 fitted with anhedral wingtips.

VL892 flying over Wolverhampton, with the Mamba engine and all-glazed canopy.

Above and below: VL892 fitted with the new streamlined rear canopy, half metal at this stage.

Above and below: Air-to-air pictures of VL892, possibly the most attractive of all the Balliols.

Folding the wings also provided access to the .303in Browning machine gun fitted to the port wing, and the G.45 gun camera fitted to the starboard wing. The aircraft could also carry 45-gallon drop tanks outboard of the wing fold, a pair of rocket rails under each outer wing, and racks for four practice bombs under each inner wing.

The T.2 was 1 foot and 5 inches shorter than the T.1, but heavier, weighing in at 8,175 lb against the 7,860 lb of the Mamba-powered aircraft. Endurance was increased from 2½ to 3 hours. With Neale recovering from his broken leg, it fell to his assistant, Peter Tisshaw, to pilot the Balliol T.2's first flight. This took place on 10 July 1948 at Pendeford, so the Balliol once more beat the rival Athena to the air—Athena T.2 VW890 did not fly until 1st August.

Peter Tisshaw was a young test pilot, born in 1923, and had served as a flying instructor during the Second World War. He obtained his 'B' Licence and his Second Navigator's Licence with Straight Aviation after leaving the RAF, and had joined Boulton Paul in August 1947, to replace John Oliver Lancaster as Neale's assistant. 'Jo' Lancaster had moved on to Armstrong-Whitworth at Coventry.

Like the other Balliols, the T.2 proved to have good handling qualities and VW897 was exhibited at the Society of British Aerospace Companies (SBAC) Show at Farnborough, where Tisshaw gave a precise and polished performance. Once his leg had healed, Neale returned to flying duties, and the second prototype VW898 flew for the first time in December 1948 (the third prototype having already flown in November). One problem had arisen, in that elevator reversal occurred above 320 mph in an out-of-trim dive.

On 3 February 1949, Neale and Tisshaw took VW897 to altitude and dived at over 400 mph to check the control responses. The windscreen disintegrated, both men were instantly killed, and the aircraft crashed at Coven, a mile from the Wolverhampton airfield. A dark cloud fell over the factory as the news spread. The aircraft's remnants were returned to the flight shed and pieces of the canopy put back together, in a vain attempt to ascertain the cause of the crash and possibly confirm suspicions of bird strike. The Accidents Branch Inspector sought the help of Farnborough, and detailed examination of the remains of the windscreen found no evidence of an external strike. However, there was clear evidence that the port windscreen panel had collapsed due to air pressure, and that the calculations used in its design had left it insufficiently robust. Subsequent Balliol screens were all strengthened.

Flt Lt Alexander Ewart Gunn, usually known as 'Ben' Gunn after the Treasure Island character, was transferred from the A&AEE at Boscombe Down—where he had been involved in the advanced trainer assessment—to continue flight testing. He was quickly offered the post of Chief Test Pilot by J. D. North, but pointed out that, as a serving RAF officer, he could not accept. He then witnessed power in action, when North phoned Derek Isles, Boulton Paul's representative in London, and told him to get Gunn out of the RAF. The RAF pointed out that they had actually not seen Flt Lt Gunn since the crossing of the Rhine, as he had gone to the Empire Test Pilot's School and then on to Boscombe Down. Twenty-four hours later, he was a civilian again, and Chief Test Pilot of Boulton Paul Aircraft.

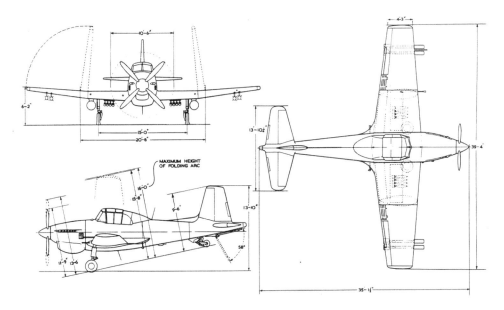

General arrangement drawing for the Balliol T.2 from the Boulton Paul brochure. Length was 35 feet and 1.5 inches, span 39 feet and 4 inches, height 12 feet and 6 inches, and wing area 250 square feet; weight 6730 lb empty and 8,410 lb loaded.

Merlin-powered Balliol prototype, VW897, under construction.

Balliol T.2's undercarriage retraction test. Behind it stands the Martinet RG907, waiting for the return of its Mercury engine.

The .303in Browning machine gun attached to the starboard inner wing.

A fuel tank being slid into the wing of VW892, the first Balliol T.2 prototype.

The Balliol T.2 prototype at the SBAC Show Farnborough.

The Balliol T.2 prototype, VW897, fatefully signed by Robin Lindsay Neale with the comment, 'Has dived at 470 mph—some trainer!'

The crash site of VW897 at Coven, near Wolverhampton.

Ben Gunn leaning on the propeller of a Balliol, having just become Boulton Paul's new Chief Test Pilot.

The Balliol's control reversal problems were solved, or at least had its effects delayed beyond the maximum permitted diving speed, by altering the tail incidence by 2 degrees and strengthening it.

The first handling trials of the Balliol at Boscombe Down took place with VW900 in June 1949, and proved that the controls were well harmonised and that aerobatics were easy to perform smoothly. Stall warning was thought to be inadequate, but leading edge spoilers installed on pre-production aircraft were thought to resolve this issue, such that when the aircraft was held in the stall, the nose fell and the port wing dropped in the ideal manner for a trainer. Top speed was 288 mph at 9,000 feet, cruising speed 220 mph, initial climb 1,790 feet per minute, range 670 miles, endurance 3 hours, and service ceiling 32,500 feet.

An engineering appraisal was undertaken at Boscombe on the second prototype, VW898, in July and August 1949, which reported favourably on the interchangeable components and built-in jacking and slinging points. Access was reported to be good throughout, except for reaching the starter motor and other equipment behind the engine. Though Boulton Paul chose to make the Balliol an all-pneumatic aircraft and claimed that it was easier to service than hydraulics would have been, airframe fitters remarked that, in practice, it was much harder to find a leak in a pneumatic system.

On 22 April 1949, VW898 left for Khartoum on its tropical trials with Sqn Ldr P. P. C. Barthropp as pilot, and Sqn Ldr D. M. T. McRae as navigator. The flight went via Istres, Tunis, Castell Benitio, Bebina, El Adem, Fayid, and Wadi Halfa, and carried Tempest II 45-gallon drop tanks. A distance of 3,373 miles was covered in 17 hours and 40 minutes' flying time. After Khartoum, the aircraft flew on to Nairobi on 14th May to undertake high-altitude trials. The return flight commenced on 12th June.

In August, the Balliol was entered into the Air League Challenge Trophy Air Race at Castle Bromwich, which was for piston-engine aircraft with a top speed in excess of 250 mph. Despite being handicapped, this was perhaps the nearest thing to the National Unlimited Class races in America—where ex-Second-World-War fighters would battle it out—to be held in Britain. The entries for this race were largely some of the latest military prototypes. The Balliol, flown by Ben Gunn, was up against a Short Sturgeon, De Havilland Hornet, Blackburn Firebrand, Hawker Sea Fury trainer, and Spitfire V. Unfortunately, Gunn temporarily lost his way on the first lap and was overtaken by all the others; he finished with an average speed of 234 mph. The Firebrand won with an average of 302 mph, and the fastest contender was the Hornet at 352 mph.

During flight trials it was found that the Balliol tended to induce an unpleasant pitching motion after the fourth turn of a spin, but Gunn took one through eighteen turns of a spin over Boscombe Down to prove that it was quite safe. Still in the running for an RAF order, an Avro Athena was rushed to Boscombe; but when it lost part of its fin and rudder during the first turn of a spin, it rather sealed its fate. Like two peas in a pod, the Balliol and Athena were so close in all respects that the outcome of their rivalry hinged on the smallest of details.

John Freeman MP, Joint Parliamentary Secretary to the Ministry of Supply, inspecting a Balliol prototype on 27 October 1948 during a tour of the factory.

Early in 1950, an initial production order was placed with Boulton Paul for 100 Balliol T.2s. Only fifteen of the seventeen Athenas in pre-production—aside from the seven prototypes—were completed, and these were to serve with the RAF Flying College at Manby.

On 16 September 1950, Boulton Paul again entered the Balliol into a competition—at the Daily Express South Coast Air Race, with the pre-production aircraft VR602. Competitors flew from Hurn Airport, Bournemouth, to Herne Bay in Kent, covering a distance of about 200 miles along the coast. Spectators gathered on promenades and piers. The race was handicapped, and although there were seventy-five entries, only sixty-seven started and sixty-one finished. The Balliol was handicapped as the fastest in the race apart from a Hurricane and a Halifax, and, to its credit, came in sixteenth.

On 21 October 1949, three pre-production Balliols, VR593 to VR595, were

Flight details of the tropical trials flight, inscribed on the wireless bay cover on VW898.

sent to the Central Flying School (CFS) at Little Rissington for evaluation by flying instructors. The Balliol was considered crisper than the Athena, and allowed the pilot to better exploit his skills. The Athena was too stable in the yaw, and the heavy foot loads and less effective ailerons made aerobatics that little bit more difficult to carry out well. Rudder, ailerons, and elevators all had to be re-trimmed for every throttle setting and speed, but not when the dive brakes were deployed. The spin was unpleasant on both aircraft, but the CFS instructors preferred the Balliol's, as well as its night flying arrangements. Many of the QFIs would have chosen the Athena, if it came down to a personal choice, but overall there really was not much to separate them.

The Athena required more servicing hours, though it seemed to be a little better engineered. Strangely enough, it suffered much higher tyre wear than the Balliol, and changing it took longer. The interchangeability of so many major components

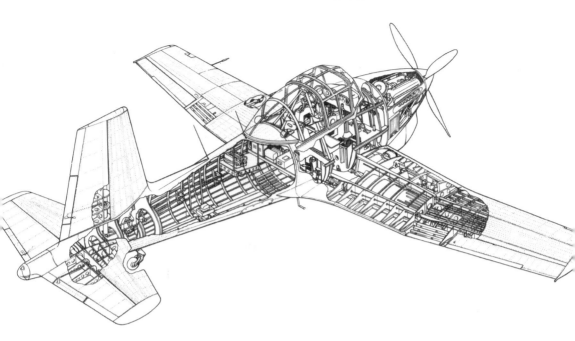

Cutaway of the Boulton Paul Balliol T.2.

on the Balliol was again looked upon favourably.

On 27 October 1950, these three aircraft went to No. 6 Flying Training School (FTS) at Tern Hill, for service trials. After this they were fitted with special '1,000-hour' engines and went to the Central Gunnery School, and then on to the first school to operate the Balliol, No. 7 FTS at RAF Cottesmore.

Boulton Paul's factory at Pendeford was at the time full of Wellington bombers, which were being overhauled and converted into T.10 navigation trainers. However, this contract was drawing to a close, and the company was able to clear the factory floor for spacious Balliol production lines in anticipation of what they hoped would be final orders for over 700 aircraft.

A second order for 138 aircraft was placed, followed by an order by the Air Ministry on 7 February 1951 for 100 Balliols with Blackburn Aircraft at Brough.

The first production aircraft, WF989, flew for the first time in April 1952, but by then the Balliol had already gone into service with No. 7 FTS at RAF Cottesmore.

Above and below: Front and rear views of a pre-production Balliol T.2.

Pre-production Balliol ready for flight outside the factory.

Balliol third prototype, VW899, which remained with the company for flight trials before going to Boscombe for target towing trials in January 1951.

Pre-production Balliol T.2 being assembled alongside the third T.1, VL935. Note the Defiant in the background.

The dive brakes first fitted onto pre-production Balliols, slatted above the wing and solid below.

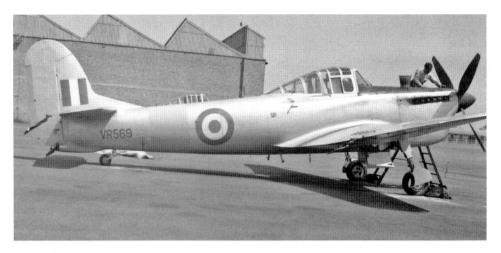

Pre-production Merlin-powered Athena VR569.

Above and below: Avro's civil Athena demonstrator G-ALWA.

Above and below: Students of the Empire Test Pilots' School visit the re-production Balliol VR590 outside the Boulton Paul flight sheds, behind which is the P.119 jet trainer mock up.

Ben Gunn flying a Balliol with a full load of practice bombs, rockets, and drop tanks on a low pass across Pendeford Airfield.

Balliol centre fuselage sections under construction. These were the heart of the aircraft, to which the forward and rear fuselages, and inner wings were bolted.

The wide open spaces of the Balliol production lines. Aircraft 14 in the foreground became WG113.

Workers on the production line, nearing completion. On the left is Dickie Howe, father of Don Howe, the West Brom and England footballer and coach.

Previous page: Balliol production lines; engines are being attached to the fuselages to the left and inner wings to the right.

2

Balliol T.2 in RAF service

The first FTS to be allocated the Balliol, No. 7 at Cottesmore, received four pre-production aircraft in February 1952—VR593 to VR595, and VR598. The first production aircraft, WF989, arrived in August, after which deliveries continued until forty aircraft were established there. It was then RAF practice to have both basic and advanced trainers at the same flying school: No. 7 operated one squadron of Prentices, on which students did 60 hours, and two squadrons of Harvards, on which they completed 120 hours and which were replaced by Balliols.

Conversion from the Prentice proved easier on the Balliol than on the Harvard. Students typically went solo after 5 hours on the Balliol, whereas it took them 8 on the tandem seater. For night flying training, the Balliol was fitted with amber-tinted screens: those to the side and overhead were manually slid into place, and those covering the windscreen rose pneumatically from behind the instrument panel, lowered by elastic cord at the push of a button. With the amber screens in place, the pupil wore blue-tinted goggles to simulate night time visibility. The instructor wore no goggles so as to retain full, if amber, visibility.

One recurring problem with the Balliol was the dreaded torque stall. When too much power was suddenly applied—to overshoot after a poor approach, for instance—and the propeller could not absorb this sudden increase, the aircraft tended to revolve around the prop, and if it was not caught in time, a wing tip would hit the ground. On 7 January 1953, a student on his second solo flight in the Balliol was landing WG113 at the Relief Landing Ground at Woolfox Lodge, and came in too high. He applied more power, and the port wing dropped; he repeated the power increase, this time with the rudder and aileron, and the aircraft crashed.

On 25th June, WG116 bounced upon landing and when power was applied, the port wing dropped; the throttle was closed too late and the landing was heavy, port wing tip first. The aircraft was later repaired at the factory, and numbered Balliol Repair No. 1. On 3 February 1954, WG135 bounced during a night landing, and when power was applied the torque stall followed and the aircraft cartwheeled down the runway. Unsurprisingly, avoiding the torque stall became an important part of the curriculum, with practice at altitude, where the effects of getting it wrong were not fatal.

The Balliol suffered the accidents that most trainers usually experienced. WG122 crashed into a ploughed field after unauthorised aerobatics, 5 miles from Woolfox Lodge; when a student could not find the landing light switch, WG115 hit a hedge undershooting at night, 300 yards short of the airfield; WF990 taxied into the stationery WG137; and piloted by a student on his first solo flight, WG133 taxied into WG186. This last incident must have been particularly embarrassing for the pupil's instructor. Further still, WG134 landed with the wheels up during a night landing—clearly the pilot's error—and WF995 suffered a starboard undercarriage collapse and ground loop—which was not. The pilot of WG209 was performing aerobatics 6 miles from Market Harborough when the engine caught fire, and he had to crash-land on a stubble field; WF990 also force-landed on a field, after the engine cut completely. WG134, which had been repaired after its wheels-up landing, was performing a roll off the top at 240 knots during an air test, when the canopy blew off and damaged the tail wheel. The pilot performed a successful landing, and the aircraft went into repair for the second time.

No. 7 was destined to be the only FTS equipped with the Balliol. The Air Ministry had yet another change of heart and decided that, in the era of the jet, a piston-engine trainer presented an anachronism. They began looking for a jet trainer, and an order for the Vampire T.11 was eventually placed.

After about eighteen months' use, No. 7 FTS passed all their surviving Balliols on to the RAF College at Cranwell, where they were to serve for approximately two more years. The cadets there faced the rather daunting conversion of going from the little Chipmunk to the Balliol; most made it quite easily, though it was a much noisier aircraft—quite apart from the roar of the Merlin, every action in the cockpit seemed to result in a bang, rattle, or crash.

There were four Flights at Cranwell, each with six to eight Balliols, though the aircraft were rotated as they went for maintenance and checks. They operated mainly from the satellite field at Barkston Heath. As well as individual flying and aerobatics, both battle and close formations were flown, with the occasional squadron formation of twelve aircraft.

There were two further examples of torque stall catching out the unwary. On 24 May 1954, a cadet opened WG118's throttle too quickly upon going around: a wing dropped, the aircraft yawed, and the result was described as an emergency landing. Similarly, on 21 June 1955, the pilot of WF995 did not apply enough power during an attempted overshoot, and the aircraft crashed and cartwheeled.

Poor old WG134. Having finally been repaired after its second accident at No. 7 FTS and arriving at Cranwell, power applied to overshoot it on 28 June 1954 sent the aircraft into a cartwheel. There would be no third repair.

The same accidents always seemed to overtake any training at Cranwell. On 19 June 1954, the pilot of WF993 indulged in unauthorised aerobatics and undertook a stall turn with insufficient height—the aircraft crashed vertically into the ground. The pilot of WG141 landed with the wheels up, and WG121, WG129, and WG123

The third production Balliol, WF991, which went to the No. 7 FTS in December 1952.

The elementary portion of the RAF's flight training syllabus, a Percival Prentice, at the No. 25 Reserve Flying School at Pendeford—where the Balliol was made.

Three Balliols in service with the No. 7 FTS: the nearest is WG126, which arrived at Cottesmore on 7 January 1953.

A line-abreast formation of Balliols at the No. 7 FTS.

all crash-landed after engine failures. Cranwell also displayed typical pilot errors, namely hitting things while taxiing—WF997 struck a contractor's van, while WG187 hit WN515. On 14 March 1955, WG130 was ground-looped and struck a bank of snow.

Pilots from Cranwell usually went for a jet conversion course afterwards—which was the whole trouble—and by the end of 1955, the RAF College had disposed of its Balliols and converted to the Vampire T.11.

Another Balliol unit was No. 288 Squadron at Middle Wallop, where it was used to train Ground-controlled interception (GCI) controllers—as many as twenty-four examples were on their books. The Balliols flew in pairs while trainee controllers homed one onto the other. With trained pilots flying these aircraft, the accidents experienced here did not compare to those at the training schools, though occur they did nonetheless. On 18 June 1954, WG149's port wing alarmingly failed in the air during a GCI near Ibsley. On 22nd October, WG184 was descending for a night landing when it had a mid-air collision with a civilian Chipmunk at between 1,500 and 1,800 feet; the crew bailed out, but the second pilot's parachute did not fully open. Another Balliol was damaged when the pilot of WG159 was giving a familiarisation flight to an Air Training Corps (ATC) cadet, and the latter pulled the hood jettison lever at 150 feet. This caused the canopy to blow off, damaging the tail, and bang about the rear fuselage on its restraining cable as the pilot landed. On 23 July 1953, WG180's propeller chewed up Auster TJ324's entire rear fuselage in a taxiing collision—as far as the pilot's seat! It must have been an alarming experience for the Auster pilot, who got away with just an injured shoulder, his seat heavily gashed.

The No. 238 Operational Conversion Unit (OCU) at North Luffenham flew Balliols as targets for the trainee radar operators in their Bristol Brigands. The two aircraft formed the equipment of the Basic Flying Wing, with trainee radar operators in blacked-out cockpits in the Brigands to guide their pilots on daylight interceptions and attacks on Balliols. After mastering basic technique, the students moved on to the Advanced Flying Wing with Meteor NF.12/13s, which practised interceptions in pairs.

Once again, the experience of the pilots flying the aircraft meant that accidents usually resulted from technical failures at North Luffenham. WN517 suffered engine failure as a target for an interception, and crashed near Shaun Prior. The pilot of WN171 was unable to get the tail up during take-off and took to the air in a three-point attitude; he also had to retract the undercarriage and perform a wheels-up landing. The pilot of WN162 was affected by oil smoke entering the cockpit during take-off, and the undercarriage collapsed when he undertook an immediate landing.

The Home Command Communication Squadron (HCCS) at White Waltham provided aircraft for communications duties, and to provide desk-bound RAF officers with flying hours. A dozen Balliols were on strength there, and allowed a number of officers to indulge in the delight of flying behind the iconic Merlin engine, which might never otherwise have been possible. Here, Balliols were the fare of frustrated Spitfire pilots who were often let loose with minimal supervision and only a basic check flight. For this reason, it is perhaps surprising that there were only a couple of flying accidents at the unit. On 19 December 1957, the undercarriage of WN139 collapsed when the brakes were applied on landing. Also at White Waltham was the Home Command Examining Unit (HCEU), with three Balliols and a staff of eight examiners who renewed the appointments of flying instructors. On a flight to RAF Andover, the two examiners in WN141 suffered engine failure; the pilot attempted a forced landing with smoke pouring from the engine, but the aircraft crashed and both occupants were killed.

John Perrot was one pilot at White Waltham who delighted in flying the Balliol. However, he discovered a snag when indulging in a roller landing, or touch and go. Upon the approach he used little power, with the friction nut on the throttle lever loosened so that it could be closed upon crossing the hedge at about 85 knots. After touching down, he opened the throttle to take off again, but then the lever had to be released to touch the undercarriage retraction button. With the friction nut loose, the throttle would then close, so everything would go smoothly until he could grab the throttle lever again and open up. The sudden silence just after take-off made heads turn on the ground. Tony Willings, who trained on Balliols at Cranwell, had a solution to this problem. After opening up and taking off again, a strong right foot was required to hold the aircraft straight; but after touching the brakes to stop the wheels from revolving, he would then take his left foot off the rudder bar, and place his left knee behind the throttle lever to hold it in place, while he touched the undercarriage retraction button with his left hand; then, he could grab the throttle again!

No. 288 Squadron passed most of their Balliols on to No. 3/4 Civilian Anti-Aircraft Co-operation Unit (CAACU) at Exeter, which used them as simulated targets for anti-aircraft gunners and aggressors in mock attacks on land and sea forces. The aircraft were owned by the RAF, but the unit was manned by civilians, including the pilots.

Even these experienced pilots could be caught out by the torque stall. On 9 May 1958, WN506 bounced upon landing at Exeter, and when power was applied, its torque stalled and hit the ground, incurring heavy damage. No. 3/4 CAACU was probably the only unit to put as many as six Balliols into an operation, or to have them return in formation and then break for the traditional curved approach and landing. All the delicious sounds of the Merlin-powered machine were regularly relished at Exeter and elsewhere in the South-West.

A number of No. 3/4 CAACU Balliols were passed onto the School of Flying Control at RAF Sopley. This ushered the Balliol T.2's last major utilisation, and probably the last accident with the type when WG217 showed red lights as the undercarriage was lowered, and its starboard leg collapsed during landing.

These Balliols left Sopley at the end of 1959, most of them arriving at St. Athan in April 1960 via Airworks at Hurn. Most were sold for scrap, going to H. H. Bushells in Birmingham, but two of them, WN158 and XF931, were reprieved. They became instructional airframes at No. 4 School of

An early production Balliol cockpit, with spade grips on both control columns. Later Balliols had stick grips.

Ground crew with No. 288 Squadron next to a Balliol at Middle Wallop.

A No. 288 Squadron Balliol, WG216, photographed in 1959.

A No. 288 Squadron Balliol, WN138.

Balliol WN522 of No. 238 OCU, alongside one of the unit's Bristol Brigands, at the RAF Colerne Battle of Britain Open Day in 1956.

WN144 of the Home Command Communications Squadron (HCCS) at White Waltham in 1956.

WG221 of HCCS at Benson in 1953.

WG221 of HCCS at White Waltham in 1956.

WN139 of HCCS at White Waltham in 1959.

WN153 of HCCS: the occasion is unknown, but it is visibly in a line-up of RAF aircraft.

Balliol WN521 of HCCS, probably at a Battle of Britain Day.

WG178 of 3/4 Civilian Anti-Aircraft Co-operation Unit (CAACU) at Exeter in 1959.

Above and below: WN158 and WN508, both of 3/4 CAACU, at the Andover Battle of Britain Day on 29 September 1958. Amusingly, if a Merlin engine was heard on Battle of Britain Days in the late 1950s, it most likely came from a Balliol.

The mock-up of the revised Balliol cockpit with stick grips.

WG208 of the Fighter Training Unit (FTU) landing at Benson in 1955.

Technical Training (STT) at St. Athan, with the serials 7653M and 7654M respectively.

In September 1952, the Balliol briefly acquired an active role as part of Operation Mainbrace. This was a huge tactical exercise, involving over 170 NATO ships in the North Sea, as well as many ground bases across Northern Europe. Four Balliols, including VR604 and WF993, were gathered by the Central Fighter Establishment and taken to Fassburg in West Germany as part of the offensive force. The Balliols were in the Night Ground Attack Wings, a squadron made up of Meteor NF.11s, four Canberra B.2s, and four Vampire NF.10s. They carried flares on the underwing bomb racks to illuminate targets for low-flying attacking aircraft, mostly the Meteors. The fighter Training Unit (OTU) at Benson also operated a small number of Balliols, including WG206 to WG208 and WG221.

In 1953, two Balliols were collected from No. 9 Maintenance Unit (MU) at Cosford, WG153 and WG154, tropicalized at RAF Benson, fitted with 50-gallon drop tanks, and ferried out to the Communication Flight in Bahrain. The ferry flight was undertaken by No. 167 Ferry Squadron, with the famous Don Bennett flying one Balliol and Sqn Ldr Barry Wade the other. A Boulton Paul representative named Mr Haldenby came along for the flight, which went without a hitch via Istres, Sardinia, North Africa, Fayid, and Mafraq. Bennett had flown over 300

Flt Lt Richard 'Dickie' Mancus about to test-fly the last production Balliol, XF931.

hours on the Athena at the RAF College at Manby, and observed that he preferred that aircraft. WG154 later had a flying accident in Bahrain, when it was stalled during a landing between 10 to 15 feet, and went into a ground loop.

A few Balliols were on the books of assorted communications flights: there were three with Upavon CF, nine with Colerne CF, five at 61 Group at Kenley, and one with the Metropolitan Communications Flight.

By the late 1950s, the RAF had a surplus of Balliols and did not really know what to do with them. The first three dozen were sold for scrap as early as 1957, followed in quick succession by most of the others; they first went via No. 22 MU at RAF Silloth, from where they were sold to scrap dealers all over the country. Among the discarded were fifteen unused aircraft, with no more than flight test and delivery hours in their log books!

3

Sea Balliol T.21

The original specification for the Balliol included naval requirements, and the Fleet Air Arm (FAA)'s specific needs were outlined in more detail in Spec. N.102. One of the pre-production aircraft, VR598, was loaned to the FAA for three weeks' evaluation in July 1950, and was then returned to Boulton Paul for naval adaptation, along with VR596. The major change to the airframe was the installation of an arrester hook, for which the Drawing Office (DO) produced the measurements; it then handed them to a flight shed fitter, Jack Holmes, to be applied. A draughtsman from the DO then came along and produced a drawing of what Jack had done. There were also arrester wire deflectors to protect the tail wheel strut from being snagged, and the main undercarriage units and tail cone were strengthened.

The converted VR598 and VR596 then went to Boscombe Down in October 1950 for ADDLs and trial deck landings on HMS *Illustrious*. They were flown by Lt Cdr Orr-Ewing and Lt Pridham-Price.

The trials were successful and resulted in an order for twenty Sea Balliol T.21s (as they were designated) on 18 December 1950, with the serials WL715 to WL734. A second order for ten Sea Balliols was placed on 16 February 1951, and the serials WP324 to WP333 issued.

VR596 and VR598 were returned to Boulton Paul and their naval adjustments reversed, before going to the Armament Practice Camp at Acklington. VR596 ran into engine failure on the night of 14 August 1952: the navigator bailed out but suffered fatal injuries, while the pilot was pushed back in the aircraft by a surge of power and died in the ensuing crash.

The ninth pre-production aircraft, VR599, was then prepared as the true Sea Balliol prototype, and fitted with a '1,000-hour' engine. Apart from the arrester hook, other changes were a propeller of slightly smaller diameter and different instrumentation, with an externally mounted air speed indicator so the pilot need not look inside the cockpit while landing on a carrier. The accumulators were moved forward into the inner wings to offset the extra weight of the arrester hook, and the tail cone strengthened. A signal discharger was fitted to the wing, operated

An arrester hook newly installed on VR596.

Balliol VR596 newly adapted for the navy.

by a switch in the cockpit. The VR599's first flight as the Sea Balliol prototype on 23 October 1952 was piloted by Flt Lt Richard 'Dickie' Mancus, who was recruited as Ben Gunn's assistant based on his naval experience as an ex-FAA pilot. The development of the Sea Balliol fell largely to him.

The FAA used Sea Balliols for deck landing practice, both on land and at sea. Sea Balliols WL715 to WL717 were attached to the training carrier HMS *Triumph*'s Flight, replacing Fireflies from November 1953 to December 1955. They equipped the Junior Officers' Air Course at RNAS Ford and No. 727 Dartmouth Cadet Air Training Squadron at Brawdy.

In 1958, frontline FAA squadrons were expected to be involved in Armament Practice Schools, namely in firing live guns and rockets, and dropping live bombs. During a three-week period without cadets at Brawdy, the staff pilots of No. 727 were able to indulge themselves in their own Armament Practice. However, their Sea Balliols were not equipped with gun sights, so they used pencil marks on the windscreens and achieved decent results.

Sea Balliols also served at two units at Culdrose: No. 765, the Piston Engine Pilot's Pool, and No. 796, the Observer and Air Signals School.

Sea Balliols were also seen at the station flights at Yeovilton, Lee-on-Solent, Arbroath, and Abbotsinch, and at the naval squadron at Boscombe Down. A number of RNVR squadrons were temporarily equipped with at least one Balliol, including No. 1831 at Stretton, No. 1832 at Culham, No. 1833 at Bramcote, and No. 1834 at Yeovilton.

Yet even with only thirty Sea Balliols on charge, the Navy struggled to find full employment for them. For instance, WL730 was first flown in 1954, but did not find a use until August 1957, when it was embarked on HMS *Ocean* for six weeks

A pre-production Balliol T.2, wings folded and held by jury struts (something which was possible on all Balliols).

to train flight deck staff in moving aircraft around. It was removed by lighter (a type of flat-topped barge) and attached to the Station Flight at Lee-on-Solent for a few months, before going into storage at Lossiemouth. It was scrapped in 1960.

Even so, the naval section at Boscombe Down were to fly Sea Balliols for longer than any other British unit—as communications aircraft, often to carriers such as HMS *Victorious*, or chase planes, and to make deliveries. WL732 was the last Sea Balliol flying.

Above and below: Deck landing trials on HMS *Illustrious* in October 1950.

Dickie Mancus at the controls of Balliol WN145.

Sea Balliol prototype VR599 in the air.

Above and below: WL715, the first production Sea Balliol, outside the flight sheds.

WL715, the first production Sea Balliol.

WL724 of No. 727 Squadron at Odiham for the SBAC Show in 1958.

Junior Officers' Air Course Sea Balliol landing on HMS *Triumph*.

A Sea Balliol during a carrier take off (which was never via catapult).

Above ,below and opposite: WL731 and WL729 of No. 796 Squadron offering practically identical photographs at RNAS Culdrose.

A Sea Balliol after an undercarriage leg collapse landing on HMS *Triumph*.

WL739 at RNAS Lossiemouth in 1958.

WL728 of No. 1833 RNVR Squadron at Bramcote in 1954.

WP328 at Boscombe Down, a Sea Balliol with more flying hours than most—482 hours and 5 minutes. It might have survived, perhaps in the overgrown scrap yard in Elgin.

Sea Balliols in storage at Lossiemouth, interestingly without their wings folded, though they are overlapping.

4

Export Balliols

From an early stage, Boulton Paul made strenuous efforts to sell the Balliol abroad. Dickie Mancus took VR597 on a sales tour of Egypt, Iraq, Syria, and Lebanon in 1950, but to no avail. For a while there were hopes that the Indian Air Force would place an order for 198 Balliols, but it opted for war-surplus Harvards instead. The company hit a brick wall in most markets, finding it impossible to compete with cheaper war-surplus aircraft, or Soviet-supplied Yakovlev Yak-11s.

When VR597 returned from its tour of the Middle East, the engine was removed after a mere 49 hours and 15 minutes' flying time, and a special '1,000-hour' one installed for winterisation trials in Canada. The aircraft was shipped on 1 July 1951, and returned to Boulton Paul in July 1952. Balliols could be supplied with a full set of padded covers for protection against winter weather, although there is little evidence that these were ever used in service.

Two more Balliols crossed the Atlantic: VR600 and VR601. For six months they took part in USAF trials of tandem versus side-by-side seating for trainers, at Nellis Air Force Base (AFB) in Nevada. The tandem-seat advanced trainer pitted against the Balliol was the North American T-28 Trojan. The Balliols were flown by RAF pilots, that service being a great advocate of the side-by-side layout; indeed, all of its contemporary trainers had side-by-side seating—the Prentice and Balliol, and later the Provost, Vampire T.11, Hunter, Jet Provost, and Lightning. Only the RAF's primary trainer, the Chipmunk, had tandem seating. Of course, fashions changed later on, and this policy was somewhat ironically reversed. Trainers like the Gnat, Tucano, Jaguar, Harrier, and Hawk would all have tandem seating, while later primary trainers such as the Bulldog and Grob Tutor would have side-by-side seating.

One of the Balliols, VR600, crashed at Nellis AFB on 5 October 1950, and only its engine accompanied the VR601 back to Britain. The Americans were unconvinced of the merits of side-by-side seating, and ordered the Trojan as their advanced trainer. The Balliol had not really been in competition for the order, but Boulton Paul did offer it with an American engine, the 1,200-hp Pratt & Whitney R1820-SIC3-G 14-cylinder radial. This was designated the Balliol T.2A, otherwise similar to the

Merlin-engine version, though the length was reduced from 35 feet and 1.5 inches to 34 feet and 7 inches. Its maximum speed was estimated to be 270 mph at 4,900 feet, and it could climb to 10,000 feet in 10 minutes and 24 seconds. There were no orders for the Balliol T.2A. The faithful Harvard served the world's various air forces for many years yet, and when it was replaced, it was generally by a jet.

Boulton Paul did secure one export order for the Balliol—from the Royal Ceylon Air Force, for five Merlin-powered T.2s. To facilitate early delivery, five aircraft were converted on the production line. The ninety-sixth and ninety-seventh production aircraft, WG226 and WG227, were given the Ceylonese serials CA301 and CA302 before completion, and were ready for flight testing in September 1953. These were replaced by two more aircraft for the RAF, which were given the serials XF672 and XF673, but which followed almost immediately down the production line, being the 101st and 102nd production aircraft. After flight tests, the two aircraft were disassembled and packed into crates for delivery to Ceylon.

Likewise for the next three aircraft of the Royal Ceylon Air Force's order, production aircraft No.s 126 to 128, WN155 to WN157, became CA303 to CA305, and were packed for delivery in May 1954. These were replaced in the same way by three new aircraft for the RAF, XF929 to XF931, but these were tacked onto the end of the production line, the last of the Balliol T.2s, aircraft No.s 140 to 142, in May 1954.

Ceylon subsequently ordered seven more Balliols, and to meet this order Boulton Paul bought back seven RAF aircraft which were in storage. On 24 January 1954, company representatives selected WN164 and WN166 from among the retired machines at No. 9 MU at nearby RAF Cosford. They were put on the British civil register for the short flight back to Pendeford, given flight tests after preparation, and attributed the registrations G-ANYL-M—later CA306 and CA307. Two more, WN147 and WN148, later came from Cosford as well, becoming G-ANZV-W and CA308 and CA309; and finally, much later, on 21 June 1957, company representatives travelled up to RAF Silloth and selected WG224, WG230, and WN132 from those in storage at No. 22 MU, and these became G-APCN-O-P and then CA310 to CA312.

Ceylonese Balliols served right up until the end of the 1960s, and might just have been the last examples flying. One other Balliol appeared on the civil register when the company bought back VR604 as their own demonstrator, and put it on the register as G-ANSF. It was painted maroon with cream trim, and appeared at the 1954 SBAC Show at Farnborough, though it failed to attract any more orders. It lingered at the factory well into the 1960s, often used for the backdrop to the annual apprentice's photograph, but eventually went to scrap.

Another Balliol which Boulton Paul bought back was WG125, used for the initial flying trials of DX.3, a radar absorbing material. This thick, rubbery substance was stuck to the fuselage and much of the upper and lower surfaces of the wings, as part of an early 'stealth' aircraft trials' programme, which later continued on a Canberra. WG125 remained at the factory alongside G-ANSF for many years, and the DX.3 was said to be excellent for re-soling sandals.

A 45-gallon drop tank being fitted to a Balliol outside the factory.

Balliol in the flight sheds at Boulton Paul, clad in a full set of winter covers.

A Balliol flying through the Grand Canyon.

A Balliol flying over the Hoover Dam in Nevada.

Next page: Pre-production Balliol VR600 flying in formation with a North American T-28 near to Nellis Air Force Base.

An artist's impression of the Balliol T.2A.

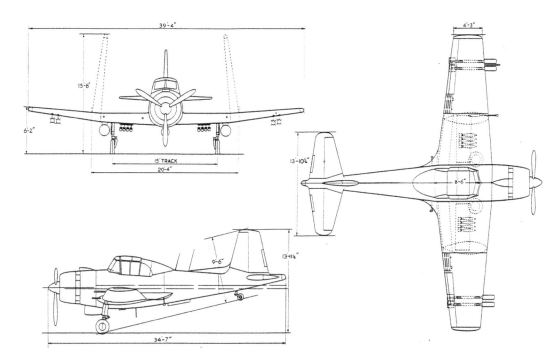

General arrangement drawing of the Balliol T.2A from the company brochure.

Above and below: Balliol CA301 before being packed for shipment to Ceylon.

Above and below: Balliol CA301 and CA302 being packed for shipment to Ceylon. Note that the front fuselage fuel tank has been removed and packed under the nose.

Balliol CA310, originally WG224, with the RAF—one of the last three delivered to Ceylon.

Boulton Paul's own Balliol civil demonstrator, G-ANSF.

Various views of the 'Stealth Balliol', WG124, covered with DX.3 radar absorbing material, including the serial.

Ben Gunn with one of the 117 Canberras he flew for Boulton Paul. Canberra conversion work largely replaced Balliol production from the mid-1950s until 1965.

Previous page: Two Balliols, G-ANSF and WG124, stored in the factory alongside a line of PR Canberra cockpits, having aerial cameras fitted.

5

Trainer Developments

Boulton Paul tried hard to widen their range of trainers with other designs, many of them with structural similarities to the Balliol. The first of these was the P.112 project for an elementary trainer, based on the Balliol fuselage but with a smaller 520-hp Alvis Leonides Series 4M engine, or with the Pratt & Whitney R-1340 in its alternative model, the P.112A. This and the Balliol T.2A were the only Boulton Paul aircraft to ever offer American engines. Higher aspect ratio wings were fitted, raising the span from 39 feet and 4 inches to 45 feet and 9 inches, and the undercarriage was fixed and spatted. They accommodated three seats, as this concept was still current when the P.112 was drawn. Such was the similarity between the P.112 and the original Balliol that an artist's impression of the new design in the brochure was in fact a retouched picture of a T.1.

The RAF's ideas for a new elementary trainer were crystallised in the much smaller De Havilland Chipmunk, so the P.112 progressed no further. At the same time, the RAF were reconsidering the use of the Percival Prentice as a basic trainer, as well as the whole three-seat concept. New Official Requirement OR.257 was issued, followed by Spec. T.16/48: they called for a new side-by-side basic trainer, for which a radial was considered the preferred engine. The airframe had to be sturdy and easily maintained, and the engine capable of long periods of ground running. A retractable undercarriage was not required, though a simulated retraction lever, together with lights, was to be fitted.

Boulton Paul laid out two similar projects to cover the requirement, which differed only in their choice of engine. The P.115 was powered by the new De Havilland 408-hp supercharged and geared Gipsy Queen 71, whereas the P.116 was fitted with the 295-hp supercharged Gipsy Queen 50. The airframes were based once more on the Balliol centre section, but the overall length was reduced to 30 feet. New, one-piece wings were fitted with a slightly longer span than the Balliol. A rearward retracting undercarriage was fitted with slightly more than half the wheel's diameter protruding below the wing after retraction, thus giving a degree of protection to the undersides in the event of a forced landing.

The top speed of the P.115 was 160 mph at 5,000 feet and its cruising speed 141 mph at the same height, and it could climb to 10,000 feet in 10 minutes. The lower-powered P.116 had a top speed of 155 mph and cruising speed of 136 mph at 5,000 feet, and could climb to 10,000 feet in 11½ minutes.

The Percival P.56 Provost and the Handley Page HPR.2 competed in a fly-off to secure the order, both powered by the Armstrong-Siddeley Cheetah engine, but with the 550-hp Alvis Leonides radial also available. Ben Gunn, then the Chief Test Pilot of Boulton Paul, was one of the pilots asked to assess the two trainers due to his great experience with the new Balliol advanced trainer, not yet in service. Trials at Boscombe Down in October and November 1950 resulted in the Leonides-powered Provost being adopted as the RAF's new basic trainer.

Considering the requirements of the specification, it's hard to see why Boulton Paul chose not to adopt the suggested radial engine, but chose to fit a retracting undercarriage where one was not needed. It may be that they were relying on its similarity to the Balliol, also an aircraft with a liquid-cooled engine and retracting undercarriage.

In August 1951, Boulton Paul completed an elaborate mock-up of its P.119 jet trainer project. The winds of change were already being felt, and in the move towards an all-jet training syllabus, the company spotted demand for what it called an 'applied jet trainer'—for armament training and jet conversion. The P.119's design did not directly undermine the Balliol, then only just in production, and by not suggesting it as a replacement, Boulton Paul hoped the two aircraft might co-exist.

The P.119 was an attractive aircraft which boasted side-by-side seating, ejection seats, and a moderately swept wing and tail. It was powered by either the Rolls-Royce Derwent or the more powerful Nene. The whole rear fuselage could be removed from the aircraft to reveal the engine, which facilitated servicing, and it was claimed that a complete engine change could be achieved within an hour.

The cheek-mounted air intakes were of an unusual NACA design, tested on a North American Sabre but more often used for smaller air vents. This was an interesting choice, as Boulton Paul had had direct experience of fashioning wing root intakes upon redesigning the ones for the Nene-powered Vampire (when the De Havilland intakes had not significantly increased the standard Goblin-powered aircraft's performance).

The Derwent-powered P.119 was estimated to have a top speed of 475 mph and 1 hour and 45 minutes' endurance at a cruising speed of 400 mph, with an allowance for take-off and landing. Its climbing time to 30,000 feet was 14 minutes and its service ceiling 41,000 feet. The Nene raised the top speed to around 555 mph, with a climbing time to 30,000 feet of 8 minutes and a service ceiling of 51,000 feet.

Ease of maintenance was a major consideration in the P.119's design. Apart from expedient engine removal, it had the advantage of a nose that folded—allowing access to the equipment there—and hydraulics to power all major services—rather than pneumatics, like in the Balliol. Provision was made in the P.119 for the

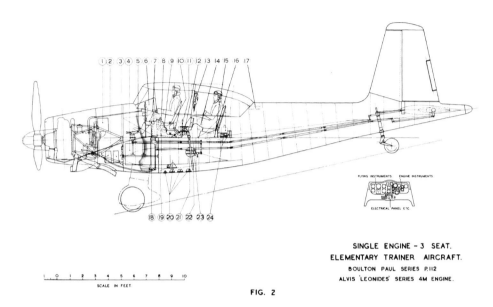

BOULTON PAUL AIRCRAFT LTD. WOLVERHAMPTON.

SINGLE ENGINE – 3 SEAT.
ELEMENTARY TRAINER AIRCRAFT.
BOULTON PAUL SERIES P.112
ALVIS 'LEONIDES' SERIES 4M ENGINE.

SCALE IN FEET

FIG. 2

Side view of the P.112 elementary trainer project.

The artist's impression from the P.112 brochure, a re-touched photograph of a Balliol T.1 prototype.

A model of the P.116 rival to the Provost.

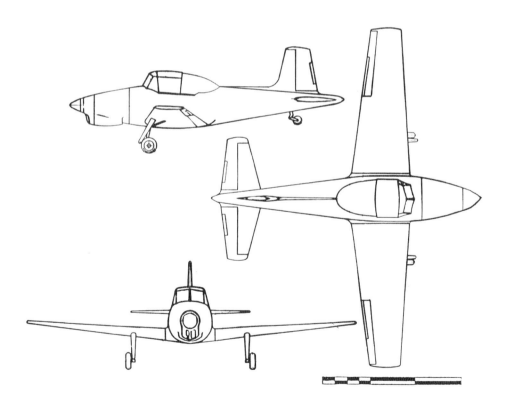

A three-view drawing of the P.116 basic trainer project.

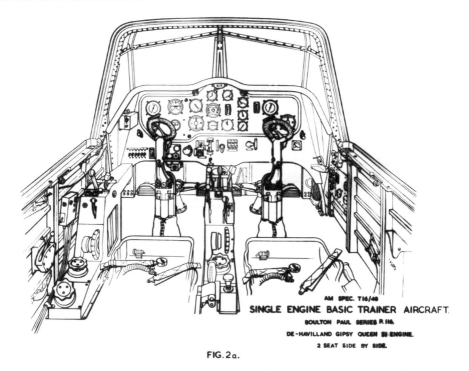

BOULTON PAUL AIRCRAFT LTD. WOLVERHAMPTON.

AM SPEC. T16/48

SINGLE ENGINE BASIC TRAINER AIRCRAFT.

BOULTON PAUL SERIES P. 116.

DE-HAVILLAND GIPSY QUEEN 51 ENGINE.

2 SEAT SIDE BY SIDE.

FIG. 2a.

The drawing of the P.116's cockpit from the Boulton Paul brochure showing the similarity to the Balliol.

Balliol's amber screens for night flying practice, and it was armed with two 20-mm cannons, and could carry bombs and rockets for advanced weapons' training. As with the Sea Balliol, a naval deck landing version was offered simultaneously, designated the P.119N, and featured folding wings at about mid-span.

The P.119 never proceeded into production, of course; the advanced trainer to replace the Balliol was the Vampire T.11, and for more advanced weapons' training, the two-seat version of the Hunter was ordered.

The writing was clearly on the wall for the Balliol, so Boulton Paul developed a straightforward jet-powered version of the aircraft: the P.125, with a Rolls-Royce Derwent, rather than Merlin, in the nose. It had a circular nose intake, and the jet pipe ran under the cockpit as it had done in the Mamba-Balliol, though it exhausted centrally, under the rear fuselage. There was, naturally, no propeller torque to counteract. The undercarriage was changed to a nose–wheel layout, with the nose leg offset to port to make room for the engine.

Four fuel tanks were fitted into the P.125, with the usual 50-gallon tanks in the wings, a 105-gallon tank just in front of the cockpit, and a 25-gallon tank in the rear fuselage just aft of the radio bay. No ejection seats were fitted, but this was not unusual among early jet trainers. The Jet Balliol would have launched Boulton Paul in the jet trainer business very quickly, had it received any orders:

Top , middle and below: The full-scale model of the P.119 project.

but there were none, and the project did not progress beyond the brochure stage.

Boulton Paul made one last attempt at cracking the jet trainer market, when the RAF was searching for a basic trainer to replace the Percival Provost. The company's P.124 project was a side-by-side two-seater reminiscent of the P.119, only smaller. It had moderately swept wings and tail, but the intakes were in the wing roots. It would have been powered by the Armstrong-Siddeley Viper, giving it a maximum speed of 379 mph at 30,000 feet and a normal cruising speed of 320 mph. A service ceiling of 41,000 feet was expected, a 150-gallon fuel tank sited in the fuselage, and one .303in machine gun placed in the wing. The P.124 could carry two 250-lb bombs, two 100-gallon drop tanks, and either racks for eight practice bombs or six 60-lb rockets. The P.124 had a length of 34 feet and 7 inches, a 32-foot span, and a wing area of 235 square feet.

The RAF did decide to replace the Provost, but with the Jet Provost. Boulton Paul re-worked the P.124 into the P.131 to suit Australian requirements, but the two-seat Vampire was chosen for that market as well. This was Boulton Paul's last throw of the dice in the military trainer market.

An artist's impression of the Jet Balliol—actually a retouched photograph of a Balliol in flight.

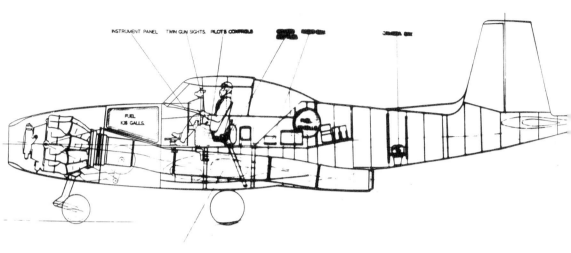

A side view of the P.125 Jet Balliol from the brochure.

An artist's impression of the P.124 trainer project.

6

Surviving Balliols

Sea Balliol T.21 WL732

WL732 was the eighteenth Sea Balliol and sole complete survivor of the thirty built. It flew for the first time on 30 June 1954, and was delivered to RNAS Anthorn in Cumbria by air on 5th July. There it was placed in storage, having flown for just 1 hour and 55 minutes. When Anthorn's role as an Aircraft Holding Unit (AHU) ended, WL732 was resuscitated and prepared for operations in August 1957, then flown to Lossiemouth's AHU on 16th September for long-term storage. The engine was removed and the airframe 'embalmed' on 30 July 1958.

After the Sea Balliols of Abbotsinch Station Flight were withdrawn in September 1963, the only remaining active Sea Balliol—or indeed any Balliol, not counting those in Ceylon—was WP333, actually the last Boulton Paul design ever built. This was in use with the Royal Navy Test Squadron at the A&AEE at Boscombe Down as a communications aircraft.

On 6 May 1964, WL732 was moved to Boscombe by road, where it was prepared for flight and eventual use as WP333's replacement. It was a leisurely reconstruction, and the engine was not re-fitted until 29 September 1965, with reconstruction complete on 28th October. WP333's flying ceased on 10th August, but it was retained as a source of spare parts for WL732, for instance donating its engine in March 1968.

Upon the RAF's fiftieth Anniversary Review of RAF Abingdon in 1968, as many former RAF types as possible were gathered to be put on display. As there were no Balliols left, WL732 was borrowed, and the 'Royal Navy' insignia painted out. The aircraft continued to be used at Boscombe after this, in spite of the Air Ministry granting permission for its transfer to the RAF Museum that December.

In January 1969 it served at Boscombe, with flights to Brawdy on the 9th and Yeovilton on the 27th and 31st. On 5th February, a flight to Brawdy brought its airframe hours up to 386.25. On the afternoon of the 7th, it was flown to RAF Coltishall, where the Battle of Britain Memorial Flight replaced its engine with a time-expired example. This was not only the last flight by a Sea Balliol, but also

Sea Balliol WP333 at Boscombe Down. This was the last Boulton Paul aircraft ever built.

WL732 in a line of RAF trainers at the 50th anniversary celebration at RAF Abingdon.

Above and below: Sea Balliol WL732 at Cosford, flanked by examples of Merlin and Mamba engines.

by any Boulton Paul design (excepting any Ceylonese Balliols which might have flown that year).

On 18th November, WL732 was transferred by road to the RAF Museum store at Henlow, where it remained until August 1979. It then moved to the Aerospace Museum at Cosford, where it has remained ever since, still in its RN colour scheme, and appropriately near its birthplace at the Boulton Paul factory only 5 miles away. For some years it resided out of sight in the storage hangar, but in 1993 it featured as the centre piece of an exhibition of Boulton Paul's history, arranged by the Boulton Paul Association (BPA). It remained on display until 2011, either in the Second World War Hangar or, given its Boscombe Down connections, in the Experimental Aircraft Hangar.

Sri Lankan Balliols CA302 and CA310

Balliol WG224 had its Merlin fired up for the first time on 27 March 1953, and was delivered to 9 MU at RAF Cosford, only 5 miles from the factory on 4th September. There it sat in store until 25 November 1955, when it was moved to RAF Silloth for disposal. Boulton Paul had sold five new Balliols from the production line to the Royal Ceylon Air Force, followed by four ex-RAF examples taken from No. 9 MU. In June 1957, company representatives travelled up to Silloth to select three more Balliols to buy back for another Ceylonese order.

One of those saved from the scrap man was WG224, and it was placed on the civil register as G-APCN. For this it had to be given a construction number, something which was not normal Boulton Paul policy, and it was assigned BPA.10C. The aircraft was overhauled, test-flown, then crated and shipped to Ceylon in July 1957, where it received the serial number CA310.

The CA310 survived to become an exhibit in the Sri Lankan Air Force Museum at Katunyake, and then Ratmalana, but in 1994 was replaced by another Balliol, CA302. It then moved to the Sri Lankan Air Force Ground Training School at Diyathalawa, and was displayed in a special bay next to the parade ground. It was examined by a team from the Shuttleworth Trust with a view to adding it to their collection of RAF trainers, but was internally found to be in very poor condition: there was evidence of structural damage and subsequent repair with parts from other Balliols, and as such the asking price was far too high.

The other surviving Sri Lankan Balliol, CA302, had been one of the original order for 100 Balliols for the RAF, and given the serial WG227. But when the Royal Ceylon Air Force ordered five Balliols, WG226 and WG227 were converted on the production line to facilitate early delivery, becoming CA301 and CA302, the latter first flying in September 1953. Both aircraft were crated and shipped in the same month. CA302 suffered at least one flying accident while in Ceylonese service, but was repaired and displayed at Diyathalawa until 1994, when it swapped places with CA310, and has since been displayed outside at Ratmalana.

Above and below: Balliol CA310 being examined by representatives of the Shuttleworth Trust in the early 1990s. The angle of the wings shows what they discovered—that the airframe had been cobbled together.

Above ,below and opposite: Photographs of CA302, the Balliol in the Sri Lankan Air Force Museum, showing evidence of damage repair to the cowlings.

The Failsworth Cockpits

In the 1970s, the unmanned Unimetals scrap yard in Failsworth near Manchester became something of a Mecca for aircraft enthusiasts. It was filled with a huge variety of aircraft, including the fuselages of the last Bristol Brigand fuselage, of the Supermarine Swift in which Mike Lithgow broke the World Air Speed Record, and literally heaps of Balliols. In May 1981, WN149 and WN534's cockpits were bought by Scottish Aero Industries/Kew Chemicals; the two planes then went to the Pennine Aviation Museum in 1982, which placed them in open storage at Charnock Richard in Lancashire, with the intention of eventually restoring WN149 and using WN534 as a source of spare parts.

Later in 1981, members of the North East Aircraft Museum in Sunderland happened to visit the yard at Failsworth, and discovered that it was being cleared and airframes further cut up. A few swift phone calls revealed that there was enough money in the kitty either to hire a couple of trucks or buy two truckloads of aircraft, but not both. A deal was struck with the owner of Unimetals to take two truckloads of airframes on a five-year short-term loan, and Mike Lithgow's Swift, the Brigand fuselage, a Firefly cockpit, and the cockpit of Balliol WN516 were duly transported to Sunderland.

In the cold light of day, the terms of the loan seem harsh, since Unimetals reserved the right to have the aircraft moved wherever it wished at the end of the five years, at the Museum's own expense. Not surprisingly, there was great reluctance to engage in any major restoration work, though the Swift fuselage was cleaned up and re-painted. The Balliol cockpit was placed in outside storage behind a hangar.

A heap of Balliols in the Unimetals scrap yard at Failsworth, Manchester, in the late 1970s. Distinguishable are: the complete fuselage of WG117; an ex-No. 7 FTS and Cranwell aircraft; and on the top of the pile the wing of WN534, the cockpit of which still survives.

WN149 had been the 120th Balliol product, running its engine for the first time on 8 December 1953, before going to RAF Cosford. It was issued to the RAF College at Cranwell on 16 July 1954, and remained in service there, coded 'A-T', for sixteen months before going to Silloth for disposal on 18 November 1955.

WN534 was the last but one of the thirty Balliols built by Blackburn Aircraft, and was delivered to Cosford on 10 May 1954. It also went to the RAF College at Cranwell on 10th December, and served for about a year. One of the instructors there was Bernard Sercombe, who flew most of the fifty-odd Balliols at Cranwell. He had been a Blackburn apprentice, and upon his retirement from flying regretted never having flown a Blackburn-built aircraft. After sending a letter to the Boulton Paul Association in 1997, it was his great delight to discover that he had in fact flown a number of Blackburn-built Balliols, including WN534, without realising it at the time!

WN516 was the fifth such Blackburn-built Balliol, delivered on 23 April 1954 to Cranwell. It suffered a flying accident on 29 January 1955, when a heavy landing with power resulted in the tail wheel breaking off. The pilot made a successful main-wheel landing, the aircraft was repaired, and it served at Cranwell until l6 October 1956.

When I formed the Boulton Paul Association in 1992 as a voluntary group dedicated to preserving the company's history, I immediately made enquiries about the three cockpits—WN516's in particular, since it was the most complete of the three and the only one with the firewall still in place. I offered to buy it from Unimetals, or to take it on permanent loan, but the same five-year rolling loan was still their only offer.

In April 1993, the Pennine Aviation Museum kindly relented after my entreaties, and donated their two cockpits to the BPA. They were transported back to the Boulton Paul factory, now Dowty Aerospace Wolverhampton, where the company provided a workshop for their restoration.

Work on restoring WN149 as a Balliol cockpit began using WN534 for spare parts, which quickly included a canopy rail, but with every intention of restoring WN534 in the future, perhaps as a T.1. Parts of the airframe were removed, stripped down to bare metal, and then repaired and reassembled. The cockpits had come with damaged windscreens and a complete rear canopy, though not the sliding portion of the canopy. This omission was rectified when the Dumfries & Galloway Aircraft Museum kindly donated a complete Balliol canopy set. This had been bought by a local farmer from Silloth with the intention of putting it on his tractor. He had got no further than cutting the rear section in half, before giving up and passing it on to Dumfries. The windscreen was duly fitted to WN149, which handed down its windscreen to WN534. The sliding portion of canopy came from yet another farmer, near Evesham, who had bought a brand new crated example to put on his tractor, but never did. The rest of the Dumfries canopy was earmarked for WN534.

In December 1997, the project was given a huge boost when BPA acquired a Merlin-35 engine. This was one of nine bought from the Failsworth scrap yard

WN534 (left) and WN149 back at the Boulton Paul factory in 1993, about to enter the workshop provided by Dowty Aerospace, Wolverhampton.

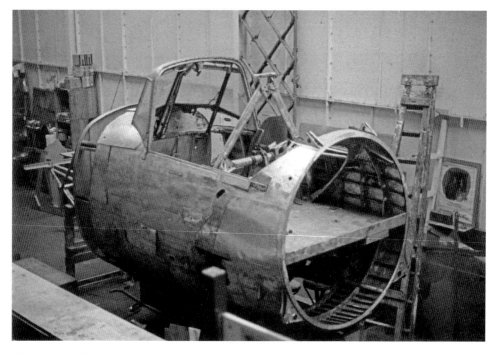

The cockpit of WN149 stripped to bare metal; a new firewall section is being added.

The cockpit of WN149 with the rear section of canopy fitted.

Both WN534 and WN149's cockpits, with WN149 itself, in the background, now fitted with a full set of canopies.

by a consortium near Manchester, which had dismantled them to sell on their crankshafts. The remainder of one of the ex-Balliol engines, still in pieces, was sold for £1,800, and presented the possibility of restoring a complete Balliol front fuselage; but the BPA Committee decided instead to build a full-scale Balliol model with WN149's cockpit at its heart, and began making the rest of the airframe out of wood coated in Alclad.

There was then talk of scrapping WN534, which I duly bought from the BPA for my own private Black Country Aircraft Collection. I began its restoration with the intention of arranging wheelchair access on one side, benefitting from the fact that one side of the cockpit was now largely missing. Restored parts of WN534 were loosely assembled on a separate frame, thus making a 'walk-in' cockpit, while work on the remainder continued.

In 2012, the former Boulton Paul factory closed, the product line having been bought by Moog Aviation from the then owners of GE Aviation. The BPA was given notice to quit by April 2013. All the artefacts, including the unfinished full-scale model of WN149, went into storage at the RAF Museum at Cosford. WN534 moved into the collection of the Staffordshire Aircraft Restoration Team (START)—formed by BPA members who were anxious for a wider remit and wanted to create a local aircraft museum.

I had continued to monitor WN516, as this was the most complete piece of ex-RAF Balliol T.2 in existence. The North East Aircraft Museum had been unable to alter the rolling short-term loan agreement with Unimetals, and so they allowed the Brigand fuselage to move to the Bristol Aero Collection on the same terms, and the rest of the ex-Failsworth airframes to a new museum at Millom in Cumbria. When the latter went bust in 2010, Brooklands took Mike Lithgow's Swift on the same loan agreement, though Unimetals did finally agree to sell the Firefly and Balliol cockpits. I duly purchased WN516 for a quarter of what I would have paid nineteen years earlier! I thought it right to offer it to the BPA on the same terms, but the committee said they did not want 'any more scrap aircraft'. I therefore moved it to Baxterley, and began its restoration as part of START's collection.

In 2013, START acquired the lease of a former Great Western Railway (GWR) Goods Depot at Tettenhall Railway Station, Wolverhampton, and began the process of turning it into the Tettenhall Transport Heritage Centre. This is run by a charitable trust, to which the ownership of the two Balliol cockpits was passed. It is the intention of the trust's volunteers to restore WN516 to a complete Balliol cockpit with the engine attached and the 'walk-in' portion of WN534 alongside it. This accomplished, they would then wish to restore the rest of WN534 as a memorial to the last production aircraft built in Wolverhampton, and Staffordshire's most famous aircraft manufacturer.

BPA member Dave Podmore examining the parts of the Merlin 35 upon its arrival at Boulton Paul.

The rear fuselage of WN149 being built up with a plywood frame clad in Alclad in 1997.

The restored portion of WN534 in 2006, the partially restored Merlin 35 in front and WN149 in the background.

The full-scale model of Balliol WN149 with wings under construction.

Balliol WN516's cockpit about to leave Millom, where it was the last aircraft in the museum.

WN516 with engine bearers attached and the 'walk-in' part of WN534 on show at the Baxterley Air Show.

The cockpit of WN534, the 'walk-in' Balliol, under restoration at the Tettenhall Transport Heritage Centre.

The Quarrywood Sea Balliols

An overgrown scrap yard at Quarrywood (near Elgin) was long known to contain the cockpits of three Sea Balliols. In 2014, these rather crushed, stripped examples were acquired locally, and may provide the basis for a further restoration project.

Conclusion

The Balliol is a little known aircraft—only 226 examples were ever completed, and theirs was a brief service life. And still, the Balliol can claim an extraordinary number of footnotes in aviation history. It was the world's first single-engine turboprop, a turbo-trainer, forty years before the Tucano appeared and therefore well ahead of its time. Yet, it was also the last British Merlin-powered aircraft, an anachronism in the jet age. The world's last Merlin-powered aircraft was, ironically, the CASA C.2.111, the Spanish-built version of the German Heinkel He 111 bomber, adversary of so many Merlin-powered air combats in the Second World War.

The Balliol was the last piston-engine advanced trainer in both the RAF and the FAA, and, incidentally, the Sri Lankan Air Force.

The Balliol was also the last aircraft built by Boulton Paul. Two subsequent company projects were constructed—the P.111 and P.120 delta wing jets—but the Balliol remained in production until 1955, well after they ever flew. After forty years of aircraft production, Sea Balliol T.21 WP333 was the last Boulton Paul aeroplane of all. Boulton Paul still built airframe parts for other companies under sub-contract, including complete wings, for another thirty years; but by then its main product line had distinctly emerged from the electro-hydraulic technology of its gun turrets. Boulton Paul became a world leader in powered flying controls, and then fly-by-wire. It became part of the Dowty Group in 1961, and from the early 1990s onward, was subjected to a number of take-overs by the TI Group, Smiths Industries, and then GE Aviation. Finally, the entire product line was sold off to Moog Aviation in 2009, and construction of a new factory a ¼ mile away from the old one, which was still owned by GE Aviation. When the Boulton Paul Heritage Project within the factory was forced to move in 2013, Balliols WN149 and WN534 were among the last airframes to leave.

Appendix
Balliol Production

Balliol T.1

VL892	1	1st prototype with Mercury, then Mamba engine
VL917, VL935	2	Prototypes, Mamba-powered
(VL954)		Cancelled prototype

Balliol T.2

VW897-VW900	4	Prototypes, Merlin powered
VR590-VR606	17	Pre-production aircraft (VR603 became G-ANSF)
WF989-WF998	10	First production batch, RAF
WG110-WG159	50	RAF
WG173-WG187	15	RAF
WG206-WG225	20	RAF (WG224 became CA310)
WG225-WG227	2	RCyAF as CA301-2
WG228-WG230	3	RAF (WG230 became CA311)
WN132-WN154	23	RAF (WN132 became CA312, WN147 became CA308, WN148 became CA309)
WN155-WN157	3	RCyAF as CA303-5
WN158-WN171	14	RAF (WN164 became CA306, WN166 became CA307)
WN506-WN535	30	RAF (Blackburn built)
XF672-XF673	2	RAF
XF929-XF931	3	RAF

Sea Balliol T.21

WL714-WL734	20	FAA
WP324-WP333	10	FAA
TOTAL	226	

Balliol T.2 Cancelled orders

WN172-WN181	10	
WN196-WN234	39	
WN255-WN303	49	
WN536-WN555	20	Blackburn order
WN573-WN601	29	Blackburn order
WN634-WN674	41	Blackburn order
WP520-WP555	36	
WP585-WP627	43	
WP648-WP693	46	
WP710-WP744	35	
TOTAL	348	

The first of two Balliol cockpits in their new home, the Tettenhall Transport Heritage Centre, Wolverhampton.